ABOUT THE BOOK

Children love to play with water. By getting things wet and drying them out they can have an opportunity to see the changes that occur when wood, clothes, and other things get wet and dry. As children do this they will be learning how to discover the world around them for themselves and have fun doing it.

Wet & Dry presents very simple experiments for children. The author poses questions and suggests projects for the readers. The readers will not only learn about the different aspects of wet and dry but also learn to influence these changes. For example they will learn that objects look different and feel different when wet. Some types of materials soak up water better than others. Wet objects can be dried more quickly by warming them, and also by airing them out.

Children will enjoy the illustrations which complement the text and capture the feeling of wet, rainy days. The illustrations will help the reader visualize the experiments.

Also by Seymour Simon:
DISCOVERING WHAT EARTHWORMS DO
DISCOVERING WHAT FROGS DO

And for older readers:
ANIMALS IN FIELD AND LABORATORY

illustrated by Angie Culfogienis

McGRAW-HILL BOOK COMPANY
New York • Toronto • London • Sydney
St. Louis • San Francisco • Mexico • Panama

Let's-Try-It-Out...

Wet & Dry

by
Seymour Simon

For Robbie and Mike

LET'S-TRY-IT-OUT . . . WET & DRY

Copyright © 1969 by Seymour Simon and Angeline Culfogienis. All Rights Reserved.
Printed in the United States of America. No part of this publication may be reproduced,
stored in a retrieval system, or transmitted, in any form or by any means, electronic,
mechanical, photocopying, recording, or otherwise, without the prior written permission
of the publisher.

Library of Congress Catalog Card Number: 70-88331

ISBN 07-057425-1

234567890 HDEC 754321

Some days are gray and rainy.
You hear raindrops hit the window.
Can you make the sound of rain?
Drum on the pane with your fingers.
What else makes a sound like the rain?
Sprinkle water into a sink.
Listen to a shower in a bathtub.
Falling water makes the sound of rain.
Raindrops are drops of water
falling from clouds high in the sky.

Look out from your window while it's raining.
Most things look different when they get wet.
Cars and trucks look shiny in the rain.
You can see lights reflected in them.
The rain makes little puddles.

Little puddles grow into bigger ones.
Streams of water run along the gutter.
Walk outdoors after a rain shower.
From trees and rooftops, water
drips, drips, drips.

Look at the shiny wet leaves on the trees.
Drops of water run along the blades of grass.
Water trickles from each leaf to the leaf below.
The tree leaves droop under the weight of the water.
Tiptoe through the puddles.

Your boots look shiny when they're wet.
Cars and trucks hurry by.
Their turning wheels send out sprays of water.
Watch out for the splash!

Over there, someone left washed clothing on a line.
The line sags under the weight of the wet clothes.
Wet things are heavier than dry ones.

10

Some parts of the ground are muddy.
Look for low spots in yards or vacant lots.
Look for dry spots beneath rocks or
sheltered by buildings.
The muddy soil looks darker than the dry soil.

Splash water on the dry soil.
Does it turn darker?
Splash water on a yellow rubber ball,
on a tree trunk, on your bicycle
tires, on rocks and on bricks,
on lampposts and on sticks.
Some things turn darker when they get wet.

Here's your friend carrying a bagful of groceries.
Watch out!
The groceries are falling through the wet paper bag.
Help your friend to pick them up.

The wet paper is softer.
Wet soil is softer than dry soil.
You can see your footprints when you walk in it.
Are other wet things softer?
TRY IT OUT.

Did your sweater get wet?
Wet wool smells differently than dry wool.
How does wet soil smell?
Be careful you don't fall on your
nose when you smell the soil.

Some things soak up water quickly in
the rain, such as the clothing on the line
or a newspaper left outside.
Others soak up water slowly, such as the
sidewalk and the street.
Still others don't soak up water at
all, such as a rain hat or an umbrella.
Try to soak up water from a puddle
with a piece of wood, an old rag,
a rock, a paper napkin.
Which of these would you use to soak
up some spilled water at home?

The wind blows the dark clouds away.
The sun shines on the ground
and makes it warm.
Puddles grow smaller and the sidewalk
starts to dry.
What's happening to the water?
Where is it going?

The water goes into the air.
We say it *evaporates*.
Water evaporates from puddles,
from wet clothing hanging on a line,
from a dog's wet hair, from your wet hat,
from wet things in many places.

Which parts of the sidewalk dry more quickly:
sunny spots or shady spots?
Sunny spots feel warmer than shady spots.
Wet things dry quickly when you warm them.
Wet clothing hanging on a line dries quickly on
warm sunny days but sl-ow-ly on cool cloudy days.

23

LET'S TRY IT OUT.
Hang a wet cloth in the sun.
Hang a wet cloth in the shade.
Which one dries faster?
Can you think of some machines
that use warmth to
dry wet things?

The tree leaves are starting to dry.
The blades of grass are still wet.
Wet things dry quickly when they're
spread out in the air.
Pull out a few blades of grass
and spread them out to dry.
Do they dry more quickly than the ones crowded
together in the lawn?
How would you dry your raincoat:
crumpled up in a ball or spread out on a hanger?

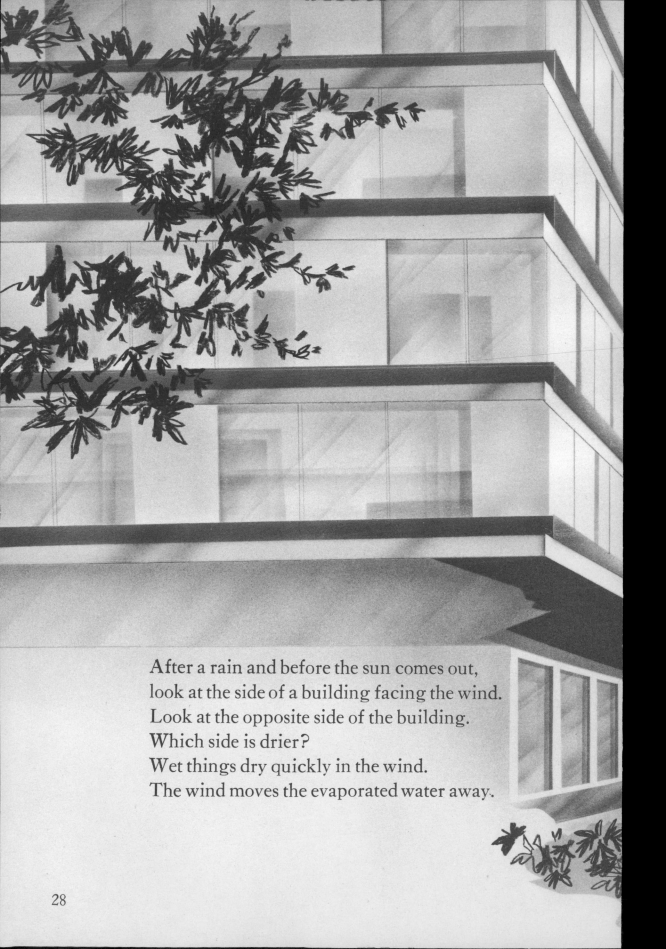

After a rain and before the sun comes out,
look at the side of a building facing the wind.
Look at the opposite side of the building.
Which side is drier?
Wet things dry quickly in the wind.
The wind moves the evaporated water away.

Wind is moving air.
Wet your hands.
Spin one hand around and around
through the air.
Your moving hand dries quicker than
your other one.
Blow on your wet hand.
Blowing makes wet things dry quickly, too.
How would you dry a wet glove?
A wet clay figure?
A wet watercolor painting?
Your wet hair?

Sometimes
you don't want wet things to dry.
You wouldn't like to eat a
dry slice of watermelon.
You wouldn't like a jar of paint to dry out.
How can you keep wet things from becoming dry?

Water Level

Water Level

LET'S TRY TO SEE.
Take two empty jars.
Fill each halfway with water.
Mark the water level in each jar
with a piece of tape.
Cover one jar.
Leave the other jar open.

Leave both jars in the same place.
Each day compare the water levels in the jars.
The water level in the open jar sinks each day.
The water level in the closed jar stays the same.
The water from the open jar goes into the air.
The water from the closed jar collects
in drops along the insides.

Water Level

The closed jar traps the water
and it drips back down again.
You can keep things wet by covering them.

Water Level

How would you keep a lump of clay wet?
How would you keep a slice of bread from drying out?
Go outdoors after the next rain shower.
Walk around, look around.

Why do some things stay wet and some things become dry?

Water Level

Now you know how to find out why.

TRY IT OUT!

ABOUT THE AUTHOR

Seymour Simon has been a science teacher for the last twelve years. He is a science book reviewer, has served as a science consultant, and has had over fifty articles published by Scholastic Publications. He has also written juvenile science books, including *Animals in Field and Laboratory, Discovering What Earthworms Do, and Discovering What Frogs Do*. A native New Yorker, he has done graduate work in psychology and biology. Mr. Simon lives in Great Neck, New York, with his wife and two boys.

ABOUT THE ARTIST

Angeline Culfogienis, a graduate of Hunter College, a student at the Art Students League and Visual School of Art, was the winner of the Silver Medal, November 1968 International Film Festival, New York City, for artwork in the film *A Place to Turn*. She has illustrated many books for children, including *The Earth in Action* and *The World of Tomorrow* for McGraw-Hill. She is a member of the American Watercolor Society; Art Students League, N. Y. C.; and Art Director's Club, Washington, D. C. She lives in Washington, D. C. with her husband.

M